W9-CTH-488

OCEANS ALIVE

Sharks

by Colleen Sexton

BELLWETHER MEDIA • MINNEAPOLIS, MN

Note to Librarians, Teachers, and Parents:

Blastoff! Readers are carefully developed by literacy experts and combine standards-based content with developmentally-appropriate text.

Level 1 provides the most support through repetition of high-frequency words, light text, predictable sentence patterns, and strong visual support.

Level 2 offers early readers a bit more challenge through varied simple sentences, increased text load, and less repetition of high frequency words.

Level 3 advances early-fluent readers toward fluency through increased text and concept load, less reliance on visuals, longer sentences, and more literary language.

Level 4 builds reading stamina by providing more text per page, increased use of punctuation, greater variation in sentence patterns, and increasingly challenging vocabulary.

Level 5 encourages children to move from "learning to read" to "reading to learn" by providing even more text, varied writing styles, and less familiar topics.

Whichever book is right for your reader, Blastoff! Readers are the perfect books to build confidence and encourage a love of reading that will last a lifetime!

This edition first published in 2008 by Bellwether Media.

Library of Congress Cataloging-in-Publication Data
Sexton, Colleen A., 1967–
Sharks / by Colleen Sexton.
p. cm. – (Blastoff! readers. Oceans alive)
Summary: "Simple text and supportive full-color photographs introduce beginning readers to sharks. Intended for kindergarten through third grade students"–Provided by publisher.
Includes bibliographical references and index.
ISBN-13: 978-1-60014-057-0 (hardcover : alk. paper)
ISBN-10: 1-60014-057-2 (hardcover : alk. paper)
1. Sharks–Juvenile literature. I. Title.

QL638.9.S453 2008
597.3–dc22 2007015096

Contents

Sharks are **fish**.

Sharks come in many
shapes and sizes.

The whale shark is the biggest fish in the ocean. It is longer than a bus.

The smallest sharks are the length of a pencil.

Sharks have skeletons made of a soft material called **cartilage**.

Cartilage is light and rubbery. It lets sharks bend their bodies to swim.

Sharks have tiny **scales** on their skin. They look like tiny teeth.

Many sharks have a pointed **snout** and large jaws.

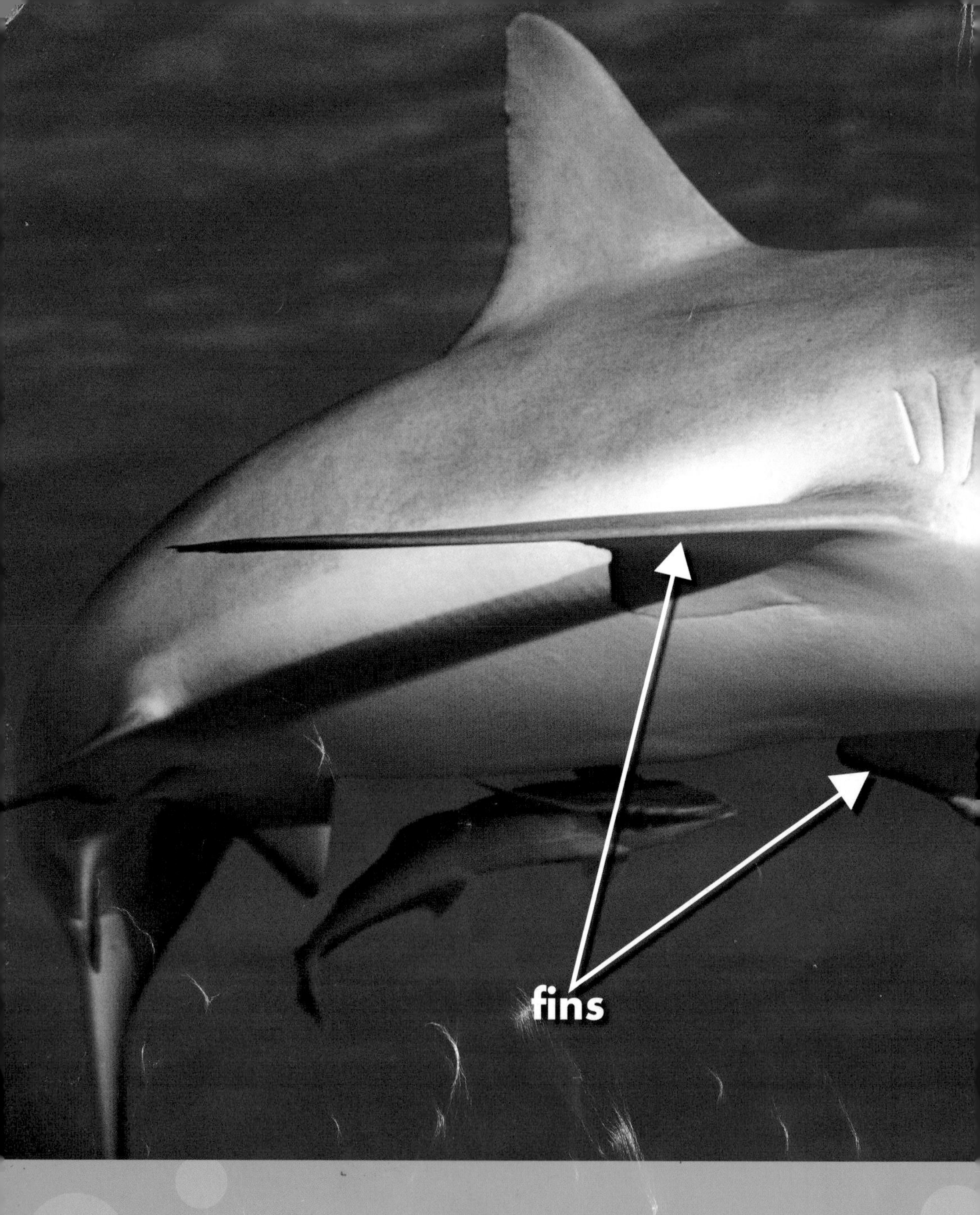

Sharks have **fins**. They use their fins to turn and stop in the water.

Sharks have slits near their mouths that they use to breathe. These slits are called **gills**.

Sharks have a fin on their backs. Sometimes it pokes above the water.

Sharks have a tail. They move it from side to side to swim.

Some sharks swim fast. They chase fish and other **prey**.

Some sharks hide on the ocean floor. They grab their prey as it swims by.

Some sharks have rows of pointed teeth for tearing food.

Some sharks have flat teeth
for crushing crabs, lobsters,
and other animals with shells.

Some sharks suck in water and use their **filters** to catch small plants and animals.

Sharks are always on the
move. They wander the
ocean in search of food.

Glossary

cartilage—strong, bendable material; a shark's skeleton is made out of cartilage.

filter—a part of some sharks that lets water pass through but catches small ocean life

fins—flaps on a fish's body that are used for moving and steering through the water

fish—a cold-blooded animal that lives in water and has gills, fins, and scales

gills—slits near the mouth that a fish uses to breathe; the gills move oxygen from the water to the fish's blood.

prey—an animal hunted by another animal for food

scales—small pieces of hard skin that cover the body of a fish; shark scales look like teeth and are called denticles.

snout—the front part of an animal's head that makes up the nose and mouth

To Learn More

AT THE LIBRARY

Berger, Melvin. *What Do Sharks Eat for Dinner? Questions and Answers about Sharks*. New York: Scholastic, 2000.

Davies, Nicola. *Surprising Sharks*. Cambridge, Mass.: Candlewick Press, 2005.

Fowler, Allan. *The Best Way to See a Shark*. New York: Children's Press, 1995.

Rockwell, Anne E. *Little Shark*. New York: Walker & Co., 2005.

Troll, Ray. *Sharkabet: A Sea of Sharks from A to Z*. Portland, Ore.: WestWinds Press, 2002.

ON THE WEB

Learning more about sharks is as easy as 1, 2, 3.

1. Go to www.factsurfer.com
2. Enter "sharks" into search box.
3. Click the "Surf" button and you will see a list of related web sites.

With factsurfer.com, finding more information is just a click away.

Index

The photographs in this book are reproduced through the courtesy of: Eric Hanauer/Alamy, front cover; Brian J Skerry/Getty Images, pp. 4-5, 14; Gary Bell/ OceanwideImages.com, pp. 6-7; Kelvin Aitken/imagequestmarine.com, pp. 8-9; Dr. Wolf Fahrenbach/Getty Images, p. 10 (inset); James D Watt/imagequestmarine, pp. 10-11; Pete Atkinson/Getty Images, pp. 12-13; Carson Ganci/Age fotostock, p. 15; Danita Delimont/Alamy, pp. 16-17; Super Stock/Age fotostock, p. 18; Reinhard Dirscherl/Alamy, p. 19; Andy Murch/SeaPics, p. 20; Masa Ushioda/Alamy, p. 21.